United States Department of Agriculture

I0420281

Economic Research Service
www.ers.usda.gov

Access this report online:

www.ers.usda.gov/publications/err-economic-research-report/err195.aspx

Download the charts contained in this report:

- Go to the report's index page www.ers.usda.gov/publications/err-economic-research-report/err195.aspx
- Click on the bulleted item "Download err195.zip"
- Open the chart you want, then save it to your computer

Recommended citation format for this publication:

Rahkovsky, Ilya and Snyder, Samantha. *Food Choices and Store Proximity*, ERR-195, U.S. Department of Agriculture, Economic Research Service, September 2015.

United States Department of Agriculture

Economic
Research
Service

Economic
Research
Report
Number 195

September 2015

Food Choices and Store Proximity

Ilya Rahkovsky and Samantha Snyder

Abstract

In 2010, 9.7 percent of the U.S. population lived in low-income areas more than 1 mile from the nearest supermarket. The diet quality of these consumers may be compromised by their food environment. Some may be unable to reach supermarkets regularly or without effort, instead buying food from nearer stores that offer less healthy food products. This report investigates the correlation between households that live in low-income, low-access (LILA) areas and their purchases of 14 major food groups that vary in dietary quality. The report finds a modest negative effect, particularly among urban LILA consumers, and this effect is only slightly alleviated when LILA consumers travel farther from their homes to purchase food.

Keywords: access to supermarkets, food, transportation, food environment, low-income, diet and health

Acknowledgments

The authors thank Shelly Ver Ploeg, Economic Research Service; Richard Volpe, California Polytechnic State University; and Susan Chen, University of Alabama for helpful review comments as part of the peer review process. We also thank Ryan Williams, Chris Dicken, and Vince Breneman from ERS for helping with our use of the TDLinx data and ERS editor Dale Simms and ERS designer Lori A. Fields for high-quality editing and design of this manuscript.

Contents

USDA

United States Department of Agriculture

A report summary from the Economic Research Service   September 2015

Find the full report at
*www.ers.usda.gov/
publications/err-
economic-research-
report/err195*

Food Choices and Store Proximity

Ilya Rahkovsky and Samantha Snyder

What Is the Issue?

In 2010, 9.7 percent of the U.S. population lived in low-income areas more than 1 mile from the nearest supermarket. The diet quality of these consumers may be compromised by their food environment. Some may be unable to reach supermarkets regularly or without effort, instead buying food from nearer stores that offer less healthy food products. Retailers may be discouraged from locating in low-income areas due to insufficient demand, and poverty can prevent the residents of these areas from obtaining lower priced and better quality products far (over 1 mile for urban consumers, 10 miles for rural) from their homes.

Understanding how access to supermarkets affects the healthfulness of food purchases may help policymakers determine the value of attracting supermarkets to underserved areas. USDA's Economic Research Service conducted two large-scale studies to define low-food-access areas and to identify the population living in those areas. This report investigates the correlation between living in low-income, low-access (LILA) areas and the purchase of 14 major food groups in order to estimate the effect on diet quality of living in LILA areas. The researchers accounted for the prices consumers face and their demographic characteristics.

What Did the Study Find?

Living in a LILA area has only a modest negative effect on the healthfulness of food purchases—a difference too small to explain much of the national disparities in diet quality and obesity—and this effect is only slightly alleviated when LILA consumers travel farther from their homes to purchase food. Even after traveling to stores farther from their home, LILA area consumers tend to buy less healthy food. Thus, as the effect of living in LILA areas on diets is modest, improvements in dietary quality are likely only with a multi-pronged policy approach that addresses hardwired shopping and eating habits in addition to retail coverage. Among the report's findings:

- Food prices paid by LILA and non-LILA consumers were very similar. There is no evidence that LILA consumers are paying more for healthful foods.
- Consumers living in LILA areas bought 4.5 percent less fruit, 2.7 percent fewer vegetables, and 10.8 percent fewer low-fat milk products than consumers not residing in LILA areas. At the same time, they bought 8.9 percent more red meat, 5.0 percent more diet (soda) drinks, and 3.3 percent more nondiet drinks.

ERS is a primary source of economic research and analysis from the U.S. Department of Agriculture, providing timely information on economic and policy issues related to agriculture, food, the environment, and rural America.

www.ers.usda.gov

- LILA consumers travel slightly farther from home to purchase their food. Almost all LILA households traveled to stores more than 1 mile from their home, the distance commonly used to delineate low food access. Thus, of the 7.7 percent of households in the Homescan sample who lived in LILA areas, very few limited their food purchases to the LILA areas.
- LILA consumers who travel farther to buy food purchase more fruits, vegetables, fish, and poultry and fewer drinks (diet and nondiet), but the magnitudes of these effects are small and they cannot explain large nutritional disparities observed in the population.
- Separating the LILA measure into low-access areas and low-income areas shows that low income is more strongly associated with the purchases of unhealthful food than is living in an area with limited access to supermarkets.

The study has several limitations. First, the survey, which measures consumer food purchases, under-represents poor consumers. Similarly, the data on store locations lack some small independent stores, which are prevalent in poor areas. Third, we disregard food choices in schools and restaurants, so results pertain only to food purchased at grocery stores and other purchases for at-home consumption. Given these limitations, the results of this study may not apply to very poor households or to individuals who primarily eat away from home.

How Was the Study Conducted?

This report uses household food purchase and characteristics data from the 2010 Nielsen Homescan Panel Survey; food retail locations data from the TDLinx retail database; census tract locations and demographic data from the U.S. Census Bureau; and food-access data from the ERS Food Access Research Atlas. These data were used to estimate a demand model of 14 food groups, which cover most food products eaten at home. We selected groups with maximum nutritional differences to establish a measure of dietary quality and to measure consumer preferences for healthy foods.

The researchers estimated food product demand elasticities for consumers in LILA areas. With information on household and shopping locations, we calculate the distance traveled by each household on each shopping trip and the items purchased on that trip. With information on both residential location and shopping outlet location, we are able to determine whether there is a relationship between distance traveled for shopping and the healthfulness of the items purchased on a given shopping trip.

Food Choices and Store Proximity

Introduction

Much research in recent years has investigated the links between household access—specifically in low-income low-access (LILA) areas—to food stores and subsequent purchases, consumption patterns, and health outcomes. There has been extensive investigation into the presence of LILA areas and their characteristics. Wilde and colleagues (2014) find a negative correlation between an area's average income and store density, while Dutko and colleagues (2012) find that, among low-income areas, there were fewer stores in areas with very poor or minority consumers.

Store density is primarily determined by population density, which varies in both high- and low-income areas. Moore and Diez Roux (2006) studied census tracts in Maryland, New York, and North Carolina and found that large supermarkets were more likely to be located in low-income than high-income tracts and less likely to be in tracts with large minority populations. Morland and colleagues (2002)—using data from Mississippi, North Carolina, Maryland, and Minnesota—found fewer stores in poor and minority areas.

Cummins and colleagues (2014) found no increase in the consumption of fruits and vegetables after a new grocery opened in a low-access area of Philadelphia. This suggests that exact store location may be inconsequential to consumers in the habit of shopping at favored stores. Edin and colleagues (2013) found that poor consumers are quite aware of food prices in different stores and are willing to travel far to access the lower prices, a finding corroborated by studies in Minneapolis, New York City, and Chicago (Chung and Myers 1999; Horowitz et al., 2004; Block and Kouba, 2006).

Studies have linked a poor food environment to negative health outcomes, such as the prevalence of overweight/obesity and associated diseases. Most have used rates of overweight and obesity as indicators of health and pointed to higher prevalence of these as proof that the food environment impacts residents' health outcomes. Holsten (2009), in reviewing a number of these studies, contends that the food environment-obesity relationship found is often undermined by inadequate data or research design. Ford and Dzewaltowski (2008) focus on disadvantaged populations and find that the disparities in the food environment along socioeconomic and demographic lines coincide with the gradient in obesity prevalence along the same factors. Morland and colleagues (2006) find a negative relationship between the presence of supermarkets and rates of obesity/overweight and a positive relationship between access to convenience stores and the same health indicators. However, significant links between store access and diabetes, cholesterol levels, and high blood pressure were not observed. Chen and colleagues (2010, 2013) show that the presence of nearby grocery stores is associated with lower body mass index (BMI) and the presence of fast-food restaurants with higher BMI. The second Chen study exploits detailed data and econometric techniques to identify a causal relationship between fast-food restaurants and BMI.

To reasonably connect food environment with obesity and overweight, researchers must assume the existence of an intermediate step, specifically differences in *behavior* resulting from food-access disparities that ultimately result in observable health outcomes. It is within this body of literature that the research presented here best fits. Rose and Richards (2004), using 1996-97 National Food Stamp Program Survey data, found that access to supermarkets among low-income consumers increased their consumption of fruits and vegetables (only fruit consumption was significantly higher, however). Using the same data, Lin and colleagues (2014) found store access to have a very small effect on purchases, though households with very limited store access spent more on canned meats and less on beverages. Morland and colleagues (2002) also noted negative and significant effects of low food access on the purchases of fruits and vegetables for both Black and White residents. Notably, the increase in purchases for Blacks was triple the increase for Whites.

Focusing specifically on rural seniors, Sharkey and colleagues (2010) found that both objective and perceived low access to food stores were correlated with poorer diets in terms of fruits and vegetables consumed. Using two separate composite measures of diet quality, Moore and colleagues (2008) confirmed that good access to grocery stores (measured in three ways) exhibited a strong relationship with healthy dietary patterns. However, these results are not universal across studies. Examining the components of LILA areas (low access, low incomes, and high food prices) both separately and together, Pearson and colleagues (2005) found no relationship between diet quality (specifically fruit and vegetable consumption) and living in or near a LILA area.

The challenges of limited access to healthful food and the consequences of poor food choices—both social and physical—have led some to press for governments subsidizing the entry of grocery retailers into underserved areas. The Food, Conservation, and Energy Act of 2008 authorized a Federal study (by USDA) of food desert areas (Ver Ploeg et al., 2009). The Agricultural Act of 2014 introduced $125 million in spending over 5 years for the Healthy Food Financing Initiative to promote healthy food access in underserved communities (Aussenberg, 2014). In addition, many States introduced separate programs to support food access. These attempts to attract supermarkets to the underserved areas generally were part of larger community revitalization schemes. From 2001 to 2011, 11 States enacted legislation to address these issues and 7 States attempted legislation (CDC, 2012). And in 2014, Maryland passed legislation to provide $1 million in assistance—including State loans and grants—to food desert areas (Maryland House Bill 451, 2014).

This report investigates the correlation between living in low-access, low-income areas and food purchases made for at-home consumption. We are able to trace the effect of food environment on consumer purchases due to the unique datasets used. With information on household and shopping locations, we calculate the distance traveled by each household on each shopping trip and the items purchased on that trip. To our knowledge, previous studies have looked only at the availability of shopping outlets at the household level. For the most part, this characteristic may be quantified by the number of grocery/convenience stores or restaurants in a household's ZIP Code, census tract, or defined radius. Attempts are then made to relate either purchasing decisions or health outcomes to these measures of access.

With information on both residential location and shopping outlet location, we are able to determine whether there is a relationship between distance traveled for shopping and the healthfulness of the items purchased on that trip. This examination is different in a few very important ways. First, we are not concerned with characterizing the food environment for each household, per se. While we do use information on whether a household is located in a LILA area to refine our model, we allow for the fact that households likely travel outside of their immediate surroundings to shop for food. Second, because we observe households over an entire year (2010) and for multiple shopping trips, our model captures how households vary their purchases over distance. Since we observe a household's purchasing decisions and the distance it travels to its chosen retail food store, we are better able to predict whether improved access to supermarkets would, in fact, improve the nutritional profile of low-income households. Because of these differences, our results may be more policy relevant.

Data

The study of food demand by level of food access in LILA areas requires information on consumer purchases, the local food environment, and shopping behavior. Our information on consumer purchases is from the 2010 Nielsen Homescan Survey, the largest nationwide survey of food purchases. Households are asked to record all food purchases from all outlets for in-home consumption. (Food purchased in restaurants and fast-food places for consumption outside the home does not appear in the survey.) Nielsen households are recruited via mail and Internet ads and are awarded with points for prizes and sweepstakes. Low-income consumers are underrepresented in the survey (Einav et al., 2008 and 2010).

The Homescan purchase record provides information on date, price, quantity, product, and store, as well as whether the product was purchased at a discount. For most products, consumers need to scan the Universal Product Code (UPC), enter a date, and provide information about the place of purchase and any discounts using a special hand-held device given for this purpose. If Nielsen collects sales information from the store where a product was purchased, the price of the product from the store record and detailed product information (size, product type) from a UPC dictionary is matched to the household's reported purchase in Homescan. If Nielsen does not have price information about a product, then a Homescan panelist is asked to manually enter the price. For random-weight items without a UPC code, such as fresh tomatoes, consumers identify the product from a catalog, enter its code, weight, and expenditures.

Households are sampled from 52 markets in the 48 contiguous States.[1] A random-weight panel (27,418 households in 2010) records all food purchases, including items without UPC codes that are priced per unit of weight. A second panel (33,217 households) records just UPC purchases. Prior to 2007, Homescan participants recorded detailed information, such as weight and expenditures, for a finely differentiated category (e.g., tomatoes). After 2007, to reduce participant burden, Nielsen stopped recording the weight of random-weight items and aggregated product categories (e.g., from tomatoes to vegetables). Participants must provide consistent information on their purchases for at least 9 months to appear in the final dataset, after which they can stay in the survey as long as they want, and some do for many years.

The Homescan survey also includes detailed demographic information on the panelists, which is updated once a year. Projection weights, based on participants' demographics, are also provided by Nielsen to mimic demographics across the U.S. population. The survey provides census tract information for participating households, from which we extrapolate latitude and longitude of the household residence.

Underreporting of food purchases is a serious problem in many household studies. To alleviate this problem, we dropped households that spent less than $250 on groceries per quarter. This can alter the sample's composition by dropping not only the underreporting panelists but also panelists who mostly eat away from home, which is less of an issue in our at-home food investigation.

We started with 27,418 households in the Homescan random-weight panel, but dropped households for 3 reasons. First, we dropped 28 households with missing random-weight prices and

---

[1]The 52 Nielsen market areas mostly correspond to metropolitan areas. Some market areas are rural and can span several States.

purchase dates, leaving 27,390 households in the sample. Then, as this study requires matching food purchases with food environment data, we dropped from the sample 906 households that we were unable to match to the census. (The dropped households have similar characteristics to the households remaining in the sample.) Finally, we dropped 737 households that purchased less than $250 of groceries per quarter, leaving 25,747 households in our analysis sample.

Food Prices

Estimation of the demand models requires aggregating thousands of food products into a small number of food groups, 14 here characterized by descriptive similarity (grains vs. meat) and by nutritional similarity (low-fat meats vs. regular meats): fruits, vegetables, sweets, oil and nuts, eggs, regular meats, low-fat meats, fish and poultry, processed foods, grains, regular milk products, low-fat milk products, diet drinks, and nondiet drinks. This classification helps to assess the healthfulness of consumer choices while maintaining food groups that align with consumer perceptions (see table 2).

For random-weight items such as fresh produce and refrigerated meats, 2010 Homescan data provide only total expenditures, not prices and quantities. However, in the 2005 and 2006 Homescan data, consumers provided this information. We use these 2 years (with prices converted to 2010 dollars using the Food at Home Consumer Price Index) as a base to impute prices and quantities for random-weight items purchased in 2010. This imputation introduces a measurement error in the price data, but avoids the more troublesome bias in prices from omitting the random-weight products.

Many household demand studies face problems related to omitted price information (if the consumer did not purchase a particular product) and aggregation of food groups, which can mask substantial differences across consumers in the quality purchased within food groupings. Some consumers may choose to buy higher quality products at higher prices and using unit values for these consumers fails to capture average prices of all product offerings. Also, some consumers may be better at finding lower prices and this aptitude may be correlated with their preferences for particular food products.

To address this "selectivity" problem, we use the superlative Fisher ideal price index based on UPC-level prices and quantities, which alleviates the missing quality information as suggested by Diewert (1976):

$$
p_{hjt} = \sqrt{\frac{\sum p_{kht} q_{k0} \sum p_{kht} q_{kht}}{\sum p_{k0} q_{k0} \sum p_{k0} q_{kht}}} ,
$$

where p_{kht} and q_{kht} are prices and quantities in household h in time t for UPC k, q_{k0} is the national average for the quantity of UPC k, and p_{k0} is the average price of UPC k.

As some Nielsen households did not purchase a single product in a food group that quarter, we need a price measure based on the prices paid by other consumers. To do this, we calculated consumer-specific market-area prices based on all consumer purchases made in a Nielsen market.

In the index, we weighted the prices other Nielsen consumers paid by the inverse Euclidian distance between them and the (nonpurchasing) consumer for whom we calculate the prices. When a consumer has no purchases of a particular food group, we assign a consumer-specific area price to this consumer for the missing food group prices.

Store Data

For store locations, we used TDLinx, a dataset of food retailers collected by Nielsen with information on retailer location, size, and characteristics. We matched TDLinx with Nielsen Household data using a key provided by Nielsen. Homescan surveys provide the census tract of each household, so we assigned household location to the population-weighted centroid of the census tract. Using the key, we were able to link most but not all of the stores. When Homescan provided ZIP Codes of the missing stores, we assigned store locations to the centroids of these ZIP Codes. In addition, we searched TDLinx data for stores with the same name as the stores in Homescan and assigned a location to the store (with the same name) nearest the consumer residence. A few recorded distances were very far, possibly because panelists were traveling that far, were living in another home at the time of the survey, or because of a simple panelist-store mismatch. To reduce the bias from implausibly long distances, we dropped all distances greater than 40 miles.

Food Environment

We use the USDA definition of low-income low-access (LILA) area as a census tract identified in the Food Access Research Atlas. The tract is classified as low access if at least 500 people or 30 percent of residents live more than 1 mile from a supermarket in urban areas (10 miles in rural areas). We used the census classification of rural and urban tracts to determine the relevant distance. A tract is classified as low-income using the U.S. Department of Treasury's New Markets Credit program, which applies to any tract where the poverty rate is above 20 percent or median family income is less than 80 percent of the statewide (or metropolitan area) median.

The 2010 Nielsen Homescan data provide information on consumer food purchases. The survey records home locations based on census tract definitions from 2000. To match these tracts to food environment information, we used access measures defined in the Food Desert Locator created by USDA's Economic Research Service, which is also based on 2000 census tracts.[2] We used Food Desert Locator data for the disaggregated measures of food environment (i.e., both the low-income and low-access criteria for LILA areas). The information on distance to stores is provided by USDA's Economic Research Service, which compiled a supermarket directory in 2006.

According to 2010 census numbers, an estimated 32 percent of urban and 42 percent of rural residents lived in low-income areas, although they are not necessarily poor themselves. In our Nielsen data, 25 percent of urban and 39 percent of rural consumers lived in low-income areas. So the Homescan survey may undersample consumers in poor areas, but these differences are small.

---

[2]The current version of this Food Access Research Atlas (USDA, 2015) is impossible to match precisely with 2000 Census tracts as it is based on 2010 Census tracts.

Descriptive Statistics

Household quarterly purchases are the unit of observation. Lower levels of aggregation such as individual shopping trips or even household-store combinations did not work because many shopping trips were inconsequential and the food spending of households was highly concentrated in one or two favorite stores. Therefore, we collapsed all shopping trips in a quarter to one observation and all shopping trip information was aggregated to the quarterly level. In particular, we created an expenditure-weighted average distance measure, which averaged the distances from a panelist's home to various stores visited during the quarter. Similarly, we created indicators for store formats/channels—such as groceries, supercenters, or convenience stores—that reflect the share of quarterly food expenditures in these channels. Just a few stores dominated food expenditure for both LILA and non-LILA consumers. The most frequented store, for example, accounts for 58 percent of food expenditure (fig. 1).

In our sample, 7.8 percent of households lived in the areas designated as LILA in 2010. These consumers have lower income and education and are more likely to be Black. LILA households also tend to travel slightly farther to purchase food. The average expenditure-weighted trip of LILA households was 7.5 miles, versus 5.6 miles for non-LILA households (table 1).

Figure 1
Share of food expenditures in top 5 stores

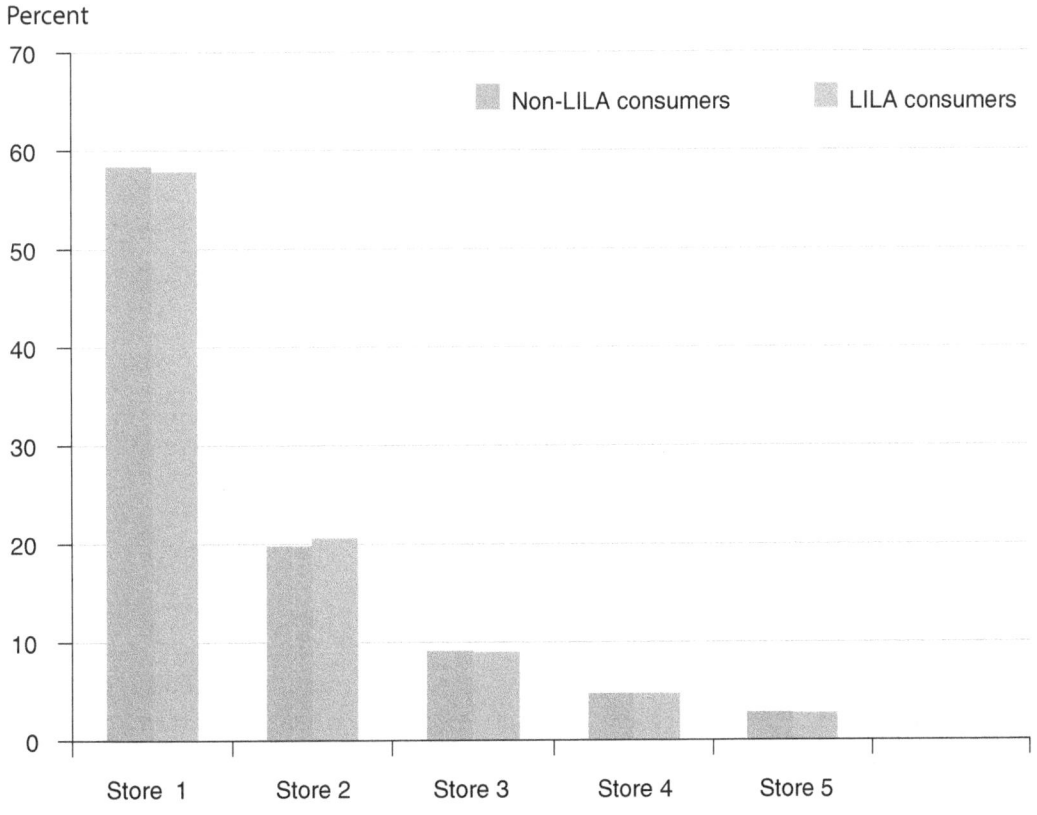

LILA = Low-income, low-access.
Source: USDA, Economic Research Service.

Table 1
Descriptive statistics for LILA and non-LILA households (percent)

Variable	Non-LILA area		LILA area	
	Mean	S.D.	Mean	S.D.
Household size	2.66	1.44	2.63	1.64
Age female head	**41.8**	15.34	42.25	16.65
Age male head	**39.65**	16.59	38.6	18.66
Household income ($)	**65,534**	50,017	47,574	40,883
Children 0-6 years old	**0.13**	0.34	0.12	0.35
Children 7-12 years old	0.20	0.40	0.21	0.43
Children 13-17 years old	**0.16**	0.37	0.18	0.41
No children	0.64	0.48	0.65	0.51
Black	**0.11**	0.31	0.18	0.41
White	**0.86**	0.35	0.81	0.42
Asian	**0.031**	0.172	0.018	0.142
Hispanic	0.12	0.32	0.11	0.34
Less than high school education	**0.045**	0.208	0.080	0.292
High school graduate	**0.73**	0.44	0.78	0.45
College graduate	**0.22**	0.42	0.14	0.37
Share of supermarkets	**0.63**	0.2989	0.57	0.3266
Share of drug and convenience stores	0.020	0.0529	0.021	0.0593
Share of mass merchandise stores	**0.026**	0.0699	0.023	0.0854
Share of club stores	**0.086**	0.1624	0.070	0.1644
Share of supercenters	**0.159**	0.2512	0.221	0.2909
Share of other stores	**0.080**	0.1572	0.091	0.1776
Average distance to store weighted by the purchase	**5.62**	4.81	7.45	7.23
Live in census tract >1 mile from a supermarket	**0.42**	0.39	0.62	0.34
Live in census tract >10 mile from a supermarket	**0.009**	0.059	0.085	0.220
Low-income tract	**0.22**	0.41	1	0
Urban	**0.82**	0.38	0.68	0.50
Number of households	23,890		1,857	

Bold denotes statistical significant difference at 5% level. LILA = Low-income, low-access.
Source: Nielsen Homescan, 2010; Nielsen TDLinx, 2010; U.S. Census, 2000.

We used the Nielsen Homescan classification of food retailers to divide all stores into five groups. *Supermarkets*—including natural and health food stores, warehouse stores, and military commissaries—accounted for about 57 percent of the food dollars spent by LILA and 63 percent by non-LILA households. *Supercenters* were the second most popular retail channel, with 15.9 percent of non-LILA food spending and 22.1 percent of LILA spending. A supercenter (for example, Walmart supercenter, Super Target, and Meijer) is usually more than 50,000 square feet, and sells both food and nonfood products. Volpe and colleagues (2013) found that consumers tend to purchase less healthy products from supercenters. *Club stores*, such as Costco and Sam's, were the third most popular channel with 8.6 of non-LILA food expenditures and 7.0 percent of LILA spending. Stores not classified by Nielsen, mostly small independent stores, are responsible for 8.0 percent of food spending among non-LILA consumers and 9.1 percent among LILA consumers. ***Mass merchandise stores*** and ***convenience stores*** were responsible for less than 3 percent of food spending in 2010. LILA and non-LILA consumers exhibit no difference in the number of stores they visit; on average, a LILA consumer visits 10.9 stores a year and a non-LILA consumer visits 11 stores per year.

Consumers who lived in LILA and non-LILA areas faced similar food prices in 2010, with prices in non-LILA areas about 1 percent higher. LILA consumers, on average, spent $698 per quarter on food, while non-LILA consumers spent $730 (table 2).[3] By category, LILA consumers spent 29 percent less on low-fat milk products, 13 percent less on fruits, 8 percent less on vegetables, 13 percent more on red meats, and 5 percent more on nondiet drinks.

LILA consumers purchase ***more*** food, despite spending less on it and facing similar prices. Thus, LILA consumers were purchasing more low-price food products in almost every food category than non-LILA consumers. Measured by weight, LILA consumers purchased 21 percent more red meats (regular and low-fat), 13 percent more nondiet drinks, and 9 percent more fish and poultry. Only in three categories—fruits, sweets, and low-fat milk products—did non-LILA consumers purchase significantly more food than LILA consumers.

Regional studies on whether the poor face higher food costs are inconclusive (Beaulac et al. 2009; Ver Ploeg et al., 2009) Kristjansson et al. 2009, USDA, Ver Ploeg et al. 2009. Even less evidence exists on the prices faced by consumers in LILA areas. The poor tend to purchase similar products at lower prices than other consumers (Broda et al., 2009). So prices in the immediate neighborhood may not provide useful information if consumers are willing to travel for lower prices. Our results suggest that LILA consumers face similar prices, but choose to buy cheaper products (within a food group) than non-LILA consumers.

---

[3]This is lower than the $906 quarterly expenditures estimated by the Consumer Expenditure Survey in 2010. The difference is probably due to the differences in sample composition and participants' reporting practices in the two surveys (U.S. Department of Labor, 2011).

Table 2

Descriptive statistics for food purchases in LILA and non-LILA markets

		Non-LILA area		LILA area	
Variable name		Mean	S.D.	Mean	S.D.
Price of (percent)	Fruits	1.00	0.14	1.00	0.15
	Vegetables	1.00	0.13	1.00	0.13
	Sweets	1.01	0.11	1.00	0.11
	Oils, nuts	1.01	0.15	1.00	0.14
	Eggs	1.01	0.17	1.01	0.17
	Regular meats	1.01	0.15	1.00	0.15
	Low-fat meats	1.01	0.16	1.01	0.17
	Fish, poultry	1.01	0.17	1.00	0.18
	Processed foods	1.01	0.10	1.00	0.10
	Grains	1.01	0.11	1.00	0.13
	Regular milk products	1.01	0.11	1.00	0.11
	Low-fat milk products	1.01	0.16	1.01	0.17
	Diet drinks	1.01	0.14	1.00	0.16
	Nondiet drinks	1.01	0.18	1.00	0.20
Quantity of (oz)	Fruits	897	873	825	871
	Vegetables	788	680	789	723
	Sweets	883	1594	848	951
	Oils, nuts	128	158	134	185
	Eggs	108	119	112	132
	Regular meats	165	192	210	299
	Low-fat meats	30	53	32	62
	Fish, poultry	67	102	73	117
	Processed foods	2,353	2,320	2,414	2,297
	Grains	454	335	456	390
	Regular milk products	806	896	866	1019
	Low-fat milk products	483	787	389	794
	Diet drinks	1,462	2,095	1,447	2,288
	Nondiet drinks	1,560	1,918	1,802	2,505
Expenditures on ($)	Fruits	53.6	52.7	47.4	48.2
	Vegetables	53.4	48.1	49.3	41.5
	Sweets	88.7	88.1	84.0	71.4
	Oils, nuts	18.9	22.7	17.9	22.4
	Eggs	6.7	7.3	6.9	8.2
	Regular meats	29.1	29.2	33.3	36.0
	Low-fat meats	7.1	12.2	7.1	12.3
	Fish, poultry	13.5	19.9	13.5	21.1
	Processed foods	257.9	183.8	247.1	178.3
	Grains	51.6	36.9	48.4	40.7

continued—

	Expenditures on ($)				
Expenditures on ($)	Regular milk products	**59.0**	44.7	56.6	48.2
	Low-fat milk products	**19.4**	25.7	15.1	23.3
	Diet drinks	**35.7**	42.1	33.5	42.0
	Nondiet drinks	**34.9**	42.8	37.3	47.6
Total expenditures		**729.6**	397.1	697.5	396.6

Bold indicates statistically significant difference at 5% level. LILA = Low-income, low-access.
Source: Nielsen Homescan Data 2010.

Exact Affine Stone Index Demand Model

We estimate demand using the censored Exact Affine Stone Index (EASI) Implicit Marshallian Demand system (Lewbel and Pendakur 2009; Zhen et al., 2013). The EASI model is an improvement over traditional demand models like the Almost Ideal Demand model as it allows easy incorporation of demographic variables in the demand system, accounting for unobserved preference heterogeneity, and highly nonlinear Engel curves. The original EASI model was modified by Zhen and colleagues (2013) to allow for censoring of households with zero consumption of some products.

Let a consumer maximize his/her utility by choosing over a vector of J-products that results in the budget shares $w = [w^1, ..., w^J]$. The choice is constrained by the vector of prices $p = [p^1, ..., p^J]$ and by the total amount of nominal expenditures x. The consumer minimizes a cost function $C(p,u) = x$ to reach a target utility level u. From this minimization of cost, we can derive a Hicksian budget share demand function that depends on utility and prices: $w^j = w^j(p,u)$. Hicksian demand is useful in measuring welfare changes as it allows the measurement of utility. However, the utility is difficult to observe in reality where we usually observe paired quantities and prices. The relationship between the prices and quantities is described by a Marshallian demand function where the consumer maximizes utility while being constrained by prices and expenditures $w^j = w^j(p,x)$. The Implicit Marshallian demand proposed by Lewbel and Pendakur (2009) depends not only on prices and expenditures, but also on budget shares: $w^j = w^j(p,x,w)$. The implicit Marshallian demand function is flexible enough to allow for nonlinear Engel curves and random utility parameters, which account for preference heterogeneity. The price of this flexibility is that there are budget shares on both sides of the demand function. This introduces endogeneity in the model, which requires instruments to address.

The Hicksian demand $w^j = w^j(p,u)$ is derived from Shephard's Lemma $w^j(p,u) = \partial C(p,u)/\partial p^j$. We can preserve the general structure of the Hicksian demand, while substituting a function of prices, expenditures, and budget shares for the generally unobserved utility. Lewbel and Pendakur (2009) propose a simple and flexible Hicksean budget share demand function that is unrelated to goods: $w^j(p,u) = m^j(u)$. Then the cost function should be $\ln C(p,u) = u + \sum_{j=1}^{J} m^j(u) \ln p^j$. Knowing the budget shares, we can present utility as $u = \ln x - \sum_{j=1}^{J} w^j \ln p^j$. If we substitute this utility function back into the Hicksean budget share demand, we get an implicit Marshallian demand $w^j = m^j(\ln x - \sum_{j=1}^{J} w^j \ln p^j)$. This demand

continued—

uses the Hicksian demand structure with variables from the Marshallian demand. To differentiate this unobserved explicit utility, we denote implicit utility as $y = \ln x - \sum_{j=1}^{J} w^j \ln p^j$.

After enhancing the model with flexible Engel curves, we need to add unobserved preference heterogeneity $\varepsilon = [\varepsilon^1,\ldots,\varepsilon^J]$, where ε has a mean of zero. We want ε to enter the budget share equation as an additive element: $w^j(\boldsymbol{p},u,\varepsilon) = m^j(u) + \varepsilon^j$. Hence, the error term in the model can be interpreted as an unobserved taste heterogeneity parameter. To comply with Shepherd's Lemma, ε should enter the cost function as $C(\boldsymbol{p},u,\varepsilon) = u + \sum_{j=1}^{J} m^j(u) \ln p^j + \varepsilon^j \ln p^j$, where we substitute explicit utility, u, with implicit utility, y.

Next, we need to incorporate prices, p, and the demographic characteristics of the consumers, $\mathbf{z} = [z_1,\ldots,z_T]$ (in our specification, living in a LILA area will be one of the z's), where $z_1 = 1$ serving as a constant term. This exercise produces an Exact Affine Store Index with a cost function:

$$\ln C(\boldsymbol{p},y,z,\varepsilon) = y + \sum_{j=1}^{J} m^j(y,z) \ln p^j + \frac{1}{2}\sum_{j=1}^{J}\sum_{k=1}^{J} a^{jk} \ln p^j \ln p^k + \sum_{t=1}^{T} g_t^j z_t \ln p^j$$
$$+ \sum_{j=1}^{J} \varepsilon^j \ln p^j$$

and a Hicksian budget share equation:

$$w_{hjt}^* = \sum_{j=1}^{J} a_{ij} \ln p_{hjt} + \sum_{r=1}^{L} b_r^i y_{ht}^r + \sum_{k=1}^{K} g_{ik} z_{hkt} + u_{hit}$$
$$h=1,\ldots,H; j=1,\ldots,J; t=1,\ldots,T$$

where w_{hjt}^* is the latent budget share, which is related to the observed share as $w_{hjt} = \max(w_{hit}^*, 0)$, and p_{hjt} is the a price index of product j for household h in time period t. H is the total number of households, J is the number of food groups, and the Jth good is used as a numeraire. y_{ht} is a Stone price index of food expenditures $y_{ht} = \ln x_{ht} - \sum_{j=1}^{J} w_{hjt} \ln p_{hjt}$. The model allows for non-linear Engel curves by choosing $L > 1$. After a few tries, we chose $L=3$; for values of $L>3$, the estimation failed because of nonpositive definite variance-covariance matrix. We believe that a cubic polynomial is sufficiently flexible to measure the Engel curve. z_{hkt} is a set of household characteristics k for household h in time period t. z_{hkt} is a demand shifter such as demographics or food environment; one of the demand shifters is a constant term. We follow Zhen et al. (2010) by using Amemiya's generalized least squares, AGLS estimator for censored equation (Amemiya, 1979; Newey, 1987). We choose $L=3$ since any higher order utility polynomial introduces multi-collinearity. The formulas to calculate demand elasticities are presented in the appendix.

Results

In table 3, we present results of the estimated elasticities of the baseline model. All own-price elasticities are negative, validating the demand estimation. The own-price elasticities ranged from -0.46 for grains to -0.76 for nondiet drinks. Own-price elasticities for LILA and non-LILA consumers, estimated separately, were very similar and not presented here.

Low-Income, Low-Access Areas and Distance to Retail Foodstores

In table 4, we present our baseline model of the demand elasticities with respect to unit changes in the explanatory variables. All coefficients in the model are statistically significant, so we will discuss magnitudes only. Given the structure of the z-variables, our baseline household is non-Hispanic White or Asian, lives in a rural non-LILA area, has no children, and has a high school education.

Living in a LILA area is associated with a less healthy diet. Consumers who lived in these areas purchased 4.3 percent fewer fruits, 2.4 percent fewer vegetables, 8.6 percent more red meat, 10.4 percent less low-fat milk products, 5.2 percent more diet drinks, and 2.6 percent more nondiet drinks in 2010. While statistically significant, the magnitudes of the differences between LILA and non-LILA consumers are modest.

Other demographic variables have much larger effects on food purchases than LILA residence. For example, consumers with children under age 7 purchased 23 percent more fruits than consumers with no children. Black consumers bought 31 percent more red meat and 35 percent more nondiet drinks than White/Asian consumers. College-educated consumers purchased 19 percent more fruit than consumers who only graduated from high school; urban consumers purchased 17 percent less red meat than rural consumers.

Table 5 presents the effect of expenditure-weighted average shopping trip distance on food purchases. Specification 1 presents results from the baseline model discussed earlier. Specification 2 adds average distance traveled to the store, with a column showing the effect on food purchases of increasing the average distance traveled in the (reporting) quarter by 1 mile. Traveling farther has only a modest effect on purchases, the largest being an increase in purchases of oils/nuts by 0.77 percent/mile traveled and a decrease in purchases of low-fat red meats by 0.77 percent per mile.

In the third specification, we interact the LILA indicator with the distance variable to test whether the diet of LILA consumers improves (more than the diet of non-LILA consumers would) by travelling farther from home. This hypothesis is weakly supported by the results. If LILA households travel 1 extra mile to the store, they tend to increase purchases of fruits (0.42 percent/mile), vegetables (0.55 percent/mile), low-fat milk products (0.61 percent/mile) and fish/poultry (0.67 percent/mile). At the same time, LILA consumers reduce their purchases of diet drinks (-0.56 percent/mile), nondiet drinks (-0.33 percent) and low-fat red meats (-0.40 percent/mile). We conclude that LILA consumers improve their diet modestly as they travel farther from home, and the magnitude of the effect is small. Given that LILA consumers, on average, travel 7.5 miles to a foodstore, it may be difficult for an average LILA consumer to travel even farther.

The EASI model is relatively complicated, so to show its robustness, we present a simple OLS (Ordinary Least Squares) regression of the budget shares for fruits and vegetables. Appendix table 1 presents estimated changes to fruit and vegetable purchases (in percent) associated with living in LILA areas. The estimated coefficients are similar to the ones presented in table 4.

Table 3

Estimated elasticities of demand across 14 food groups (percent)

	Fruits	Vegetables	Sweets	Oils, nuts	Eggs	Red meats	Low fat red meats	Fish, poultry	Processed foods	Grains	Milk products	Low-fat milk products	Diet drinks	Non-diet drinks
Fruits	-0.61 (0.07)	-0.01 (0.01)	-0.03 (0.01)	0.01 (0.01)	0.00 (0.00)	-0.06 (0.01)	0.00 (0.01)	-0.01 (0.01)	-0.14 (0.07)	-0.01 (0.01)	-0.06 (0.01)	0.04 (0.01)	-0.04 (0.00)	-0.03 (0.00)
Vegetables	-0.01 (0.01)	-0.69 (0.05)	-0.04 (0.05)	-0.05 (0.03)	0.00 (0.00)	-0.04 (0.01)	-0.02 (0.00)	-0.01 (0.00)	-0.09 (0.03)	0.00 (0.01)	-0.02 (0.01)	0.00 (0.02)	0.00 (0.01)	-0.01 (0.02)
Sweets	-0.02 (0.01)	-0.02 (0.03)	-0.59 (0.03)	0.00 (0.01)	-0.01 (0.00)	-0.01 (0.01)	-0.01 (0.00)	-0.01 (0.00)	-0.10 (0.03)	-0.07 (0.01)	-0.03 (0.01)	0.00 (0.00)	-0.07 (0.01)	-0.03 (0.01)
Oils, nuts	0.03 (0.02)	-0.10 (0.07)	-0.01 (0.02)	-0.59 (0.08)	-0.02 (0.00)	-0.01 (0.01)	0.00 (0.00)	-0.03 (0.01)	-0.20 (0.03)	-0.05 (0.01)	-0.01 (0.01)	0.00 (0.01)	0.02 (0.01)	0.01 (0.01)
Eggs	0.00 (0.03)	0.02 (0.03)	-0.06 (0.05)	-0.06 (0.02)	-0.57 (0.08)	-0.03 (0.02)	0.03 (0.01)	-0.01 (0.01)	-0.19 (0.07)	0.01 (0.06)	0.02 (0.03)	0.01 (0.02)	0.04 (0.04)	-0.05 (0.01)
Red meats	-0.10 (0.01)	-0.07 (0.03)	-0.03 (0.02)	-0.01 (0.01)	-0.01 (0.00)	-0.54 (0.07)	0.00 (0.02)	0.00 (0.00)	-0.08 (0.08)	-0.05 (0.01)	-0.03 (0.02)	-0.06 (0.01)	0.03 (0.01)	0.00 (0.01)
Low-fat red meats	-0.02 (0.06)	-0.06 (0.02)	-0.04 (0.02)	0.01 (0.01)	0.02 (0.00)	0.00 (0.05)	-0.63 (0.09)	-0.01 (0.01)	-0.26 (0.06)	-0.03 (0.02)	0.01 (0.01)	-0.01 (0.01)	0.09 (0.03)	-0.04 (0.04)
Fish, poultry	-0.04 (0.02)	-0.04 (0.01)	-0.05 (0.02)	-0.03 (0.01)	-0.01 (0.00)	0.00 (0.01)	-0.01 (0.01)	-0.65 (0.05)	-0.08 (0.06)	-0.04 (0.03)	-0.10 (0.04)	0.02 (0.02)	0.02 (0.01)	-0.02 (0.02)
Processed foods	-0.04 (0.01)	-0.03 (0.01)	-0.05 (0.00)	-0.03 (0.00)	-0.01 (0.00)	-0.02 (0.01)	-0.02 (0.00)	-0.01 (0.00)	-0.71 (0.04)	-0.05 (0.00)	-0.05 (0.01)	-0.03 (0.00)	-0.03 (0.01)	-0.01 (0.00)
Grains	0.00 (0.02)	0.01 (0.01)	-0.11 (0.01)	-0.02 (0.00)	0.00 (0.01)	-0.03 (0.01)	-0.01 (0.00)	-0.01 (0.01)	-0.16 (0.04)	-0.46 (0.09)	0.00 (0.04)	-0.02 (0.00)	-0.02 (0.01)	-0.03 (0.00)
Milk products	-0.05 (0.01)	-0.02 (0.01)	-0.04 (0.01)	0.00 (0.00)	0.00 (0.00)	-0.02 (0.01)	0.00 (0.00)	-0.03 (0.01)	-0.16 (0.04)	0.00 (0.03)	-0.53 (0.07)	-0.04 (0.01)	-0.01 (0.00)	0.00 (0.00)
Low-fat milk products	0.08 (0.02)	0.02 (0.04)	0.02 (0.01)	0.00 (0.01)	0.00 (0.01)	-0.06 (0.02)	0.00 (0.00)	0.02 (0.01)	-0.16 (0.04)	-0.03 (0.01)	-0.08 (0.01)	-0.64 (0.07)	-0.02 (0.00)	0.00 (0.01)
Diet drinks	-0.06 (0.01)	0.00 (0.02)	-0.15 (0.02)	0.01 (0.00)	0.01 (0.01)	0.02 (0.01)	0.03 (0.01)	0.01 (0.00)	-0.16 (0.05)	-0.03 (0.01)	-0.02 (0.00)	-0.02 (0.00)	-0.65 (0.05)	0.01 (0.02)
Non-diet drinks	0.00 (0.03)	0.03 (0.03)	0.02 (0.05)	0.02 (0.01)	0.00 (0.01)	0.02 (0.01)	0.00 (0.01)	0.00 (0.02)	0.18 (0.10)	0.00 (0.03)	0.03 (0.04)	0.01 (0.01)	0.04 (0.03)	-0.76 (0.03)

Coefficients statistically significant at 1% level are marked bold.
Source: Computed by USDA, Economic Research Service.

Table 4

The effect of demographic factors on food purchases

	LILA	House-hold size	Children 0-6 years old	Children 7-12 years old	Children 13-17 years old	Black	Hispanic	Less than high school	College graduate	Urban	Household income ($)
Fruits	-4.34	-7.92	22.65	7.14	-2.42	11.27	9.27	-13.67	19.45	7.77	1.32
	(0.0017)	(0.0031)	(0.0088)	(0.0028)	(0.0009)	(0.0044)	(0.0036)	(0.0053)	(0.0075)	(0.0030)	(0.2448)
Vegetables	-2.43	-2.01	-4.58	-8.43	-11.01	-5.82	3.16	-5.81	5.10	3.70	0.78
	(0.0017)	(0.0014)	(0.0033)	(0.0061)	(0.0079)	(0.0042)	(0.0023)	(0.0042)	(0.0037)	(0.0027)	(0.1972)
Sweets	0.02	-1.63	-6.03	0.33	-0.22	-3.79	-6.38	2.23	-6.21	-1.06	-0.88
	(0.0000)	(0.0013)	(0.0049)	(0.0003)	(0.0002)	(0.0031)	(0.0052)	(0.0018)	(0.0051)	(0.0009)	(0.1076)
Oils, nuts	0.21	-5.74	-11.97	-11.55	-11.33	7.31	2.44	-14.48	15.02	-3.64	_0.46_
	(0.0002)	(0.0049)	(0.0103)	(0.0099)	(0.0097)	(0.0063)	(0.0021)	(0.0124)	(0.0129)	(0.0031)	(0.3085)
Eggs	3.37	5.24	-0.45	-7.15	-9.34	16.41	16.11	11.05	0.90	-3.76	-1.01
	(0.0011)	(0.0016)	(0.0001)	(0.0022)	(0.0029)	(0.0051)	(0.0050)	(0.0035)	(0.0003)	(0.0012)	(0.3819)
Red meats	8.55	8.46	-2.92	-1.44	-2.61	31.03	-1.61	19.27	-9.96	-16.97	-1.42
	(0.0089)	(0.0089)	(0.0031)	(0.0015)	(0.0027)	(0.0325)	(0.0017)	(0.0202)	(0.0104)	(0.0178)	(0.2356)
Low-fat red meats	4.01	2.84	13.80	19.08	8.49	-20.29	26.15	3.66	7.73	-6.26	_-0.81_
	(0.0103)	(0.0073)	(0.0356)	(0.0492)	(0.0219)	(0.0523)	(0.0674)	(0.0094)	(0.0199)	(0.0162)	(0.6247)
Fish, poultry	1.25	3.15	-13.78	-12.45	-5.36	60.46	7.79	-11.86	7.33	-0.25	_-0.19_
	(0.0029)	(0.0073)	(0.0318)	(0.0287)	(0.0124)	(0.1395)	(0.0180)	(0.0274)	(0.0169)	(0.0006)	(0.2397)
Processed foods	0.18	-0.11	-3.23	0.83	2.96	6.66	0.63	1.19	-4.04	3.50	_0.11_
	(0.0005)	(0.0003)	(0.0095)	(0.0024)	(0.0087)	(0.0196)	(0.0019)	(0.0035)	(0.0119)	(0.0103)	(0.0592)
Grains	-2.71	5.62	1.66	6.46	3.98	-8.28	0.03	-0.17	3.93	-2.64	_-0.25_
	(0.0030)	(0.0061)	(0.0018)	(0.0071)	(0.0043)	(0.0090)	(0.0000)	(0.0002)	(0.0043)	(0.0029)	(0.1459)
Milk products	0.97	3.84	17.91	-2.01	0.65	-28.12	-0.08	-4.89	0.35	-7.29	-0.35
	(0.0008)	(0.0033)	(0.0156)	(0.0017)	(0.0006)	(0.0244)	(0.0001)	(0.0042)	(0.0003)	(0.0063)	(0.1150)
Low-fat milk products	-10.37	-5.44	30.46	22.76	9.15	-66.73	-18.27	-28.50	27.88	8.22	1.72
	(0.0089)	(0.0047)	(0.0262)	(0.0195)	(0.0079)	(0.0573)	(0.0157)	(0.0245)	(0.0239)	(0.0071)	(0.3184)
Diet drinks	5.23	-4.49	-21.30	-10.40	-12.52	-36.59	-8.57	8.87	-5.25	-3.74	1.03
	(0.0065)	(0.0056)	(0.0264)	(0.0129)	(0.0155)	(0.0453)	(0.0106)	(0.0110)	(0.0065)	(0.0046)	(0.1456)
Nondiet drinks	2.61	6.24	-5.92	-3.44	10.99	35.25	0.07	24.74	-14.19	-6.36	-1.46
	(0.0284)	(0.0679)	(0.0643)	(0.0374)	(0.1194)	(0.3832)	(0.0007)	(0.2689)	(0.1543)	(0.0691)	(0.1488)

All coefficients are statistically significant at 5% level, except the underlined coefficients. LILA - Low-income, low-access.
Source: Computed by USDA, Economic Research Service.

Table 5
Effect on food purchases of distance travelled to stores

	(1)	(2)		(3)		
	LILA	LILA	distance	LILA	distance	LILA*distance
Fruits	-4.34	-4.08	-0.21	-7.26	-0.26	0.42
	(0.0017)	(0.0016)	(0.0001)	(0.0028)	(0.0001)	(0.0002)
Vegetables	-2.43	-2.54	0.09	-6.71	0.02	0.55
	(0.0017)	(0.0018)	(0.0001)	(0.0048)	(0.0000)	(0.0004)
Sweets	0.02	0.13	-0.10	1.64	-0.07	-0.20
	(0.0000)	(0.0001)	(0.0001)	(0.0013)	(0.0001)	(0.0002)
Oils, nuts	0.21	-0.72	0.77	-3.05	0.73	0.30
	(0.0002)	(0.0006)	(0.0006)	(0.0026)	(0.0006)	(0.0003)
Eggs	3.37	3.44	-0.05	5.95	-0.01	-0.33
	(0.0011)	(0.0011)	(0.0000)	(0.0019)	(0.0000)	(0.0001)
Red meats	8.55	8.33	0.19	10.63	0.23	-0.30
	(0.0089)	(0.0087)	(0.0002)	(0.0111)	(0.0002)	(0.0003)
Low-fat red meats	4.01	4.92	-0.77	7.90	-0.72	-0.40
	(0.0103)	(0.0127)	(0.0020)	(0.0204)	(0.0018)	(0.0010)
Fish, poultry	1.25	0.69	0.44	-4.40	0.36	0.67
	(0.0029)	(0.0016)	(0.0010)	(0.0101)	(0.0008)	(0.0015)
Processed foods	0.18	0.24	-0.05	0.97	-0.04	-0.10
	(0.0005)	(0.0007)	(0.0001)	(0.0029)	(0.0001)	(0.0003)
Grains	-2.71	-2.65	-0.06	-2.49	-0.05	-0.02
	(0.0030)	(0.0029)	(0.0001)	(0.0027)	(0.0001)	(0.0000)
Milk products	0.97	0.74	0.18	-0.46	0.16	0.16
	(0.0008)	(0.0006)	(0.0002)	(0.0004)	(0.0001)	(0.0001)
Low-fat milk products	-10.37	-9.90	-0.37	-14.53	-0.44	0.61
	(0.0089)	(0.0086)	(0.0003)	(0.0126)	(0.0004)	(0.0005)
Diet drinks	5.23	4.99	0.22	9.19	0.29	-0.56
	(0.0065)	(0.0061)	(0.0003)	(0.0113)	(0.0004)	(0.0007)
Non-diet drinks	2.61	2.66	-0.04	5.19	0.00	-0.33
	(0.0284)	(0.0289)	(0.0004)	(0.0564)	(0.0000)	(0.0036)

All coefficients are statistically significant at 1%. LILA - Low-income, low-access.
Source: Computed by USDA, Economic Research Service.

Urban and Rural LILA Areas

Rural and urban areas need to pass different distance thresholds to be classified as LILA areas (10 miles and 1 mile, respectively). The effect of travelling an extra mile to the store may be more modest for rural residents who typically have to travel longer distances for services and shopping. The effect on food purchases of living in a rural LILA area is much weaker than the effect of living in an urban one (table 6). Living in an urban LILA area is associated with fewer purchases of fruits (-6.7 percent), vegetables (-4.9 percent), and low-fat milk products (-14.6 percent) and greater purchases of red meats (10.1 percent) and nondiet drinks (5.4 percent). (The urban column shows the average difference in purchases between urban and rural consumers.) We find that urban consumers have more healthful diets, purchasing more fruits, vegetables, and low-fat milk products and fewer red meats and nondiet drinks. This general difference makes the diet of urban LILA and rural non-LILA consumers roughly similar.

Next, we interact average shopping distance travelled with the indicators for rural and urban LILA areas. For consumers living in urban LILA areas, travelling 1 more mile to the store is associated with increased purchases of vegetables (0.79 percent), fruits (0.55 percent), oils/nuts (0.89 percent), low-fat red meats (1.33 percent), and fish/poultry (0.56 percent), and reduced purchases of nondiet drinks (-0.32 percent) (table 7). For rural LILA consumers, a 1-mile increase in distance travelled is associated with an increase in purchases of milk products (0.29 percent) and a decrease in the purchase of oils/nuts (-0.69 percent) and sweets (-0.54 percent).

Poverty or Low Access as Greater Factor in Food Purchases: Disaggregation of LILA

For a census tract to be classified as LILA, it needs to have both low-income households and limited access to retail foodstores. In this section, we consider these criteria separately to assess their relative importance.

Depth of poverty and urban residence have larger impacts on consumers' diets than the distance to supermarkets. Consumers living in poor areas purchase less fruit (-5.7 percent), fewer vegetables (-2.7 percent), more sweets (2.6 percent), more red meats (6 percent), fewer low-fat milk products (-15.1 percent), and more nondiet drinks (9.9 percent) than consumers in rural non-LILA areas (table 8). On the other hand, living in an urban census tract that is not a LILA area is associated with a healthier diet. Consumers in urban tracts buy 11.3 percent more fruits, 4.4 percent more vegetables, 21.6 percent less red meats, and 9.7 percent more low-fat milk products.

Curiously, residents of rural areas more than 10 miles from a supermarket and residents of rural LILA areas have healthier diets than rural residents closer to supermarkets. Seemingly, the benchmark of 10-mile distance from a supermarket does not equate to a disadvantaged rural population.

Longer distance in an urban context has a stronger effect on diet. Urban consumers who are more than 1 mile from a supermarket purchase 7.3 percent fewer fruit and 11.1 percent more red meats (table 8). On the positive side, they purchase 6.8 percent fewer nondiet drinks and 5.1 percent more fish and poultry. The joint effect of low income and low access in urban areas (Urban LILA indicator) is associated with the purchase of 2.7 percent fewer vegetables, 3.6 percent more red meats, and 5.5 percent less fish and poultry.

Table 6

Effect on food purchases of living in rural and urban low-income, low-access areas 1

	Rural LILA	Urban LILA	Urban
Fruits	0.62	-6.69	8.49
	(0.0002)	(0.0026)	(0.0033)
Vegetables	2.83	-4.92	4.47
	(0.0020)	(0.0035)	(0.0032)
Sweets	0.72	-0.32	-0.95
	(0.0006)	(0.0003)	(0.0008)
Oils, nuts	8.05	-3.51	-2.52
	(0.0069)	(0.0030)	(0.0022)
Eggs	-0.09	5.00	-4.26
	(0.0000)	(0.0016)	(0.0013)
Red meats	5.25	10.12	-17.45
	(0.0055)	(0.0106)	(0.0183)
Low-fat red meats	-1.45	6.62	-7.05
	(0.0037)	(0.0171)	(0.0182)
Fish, poultry	8.62	-2.26	0.82
	(0.0199)	(0.0052)	(0.0019)
Processed foods	-1.90	1.18	3.19
	(0.0056)	(0.0035)	(0.0094)
Grains	-1.39	-3.34	-2.45
	(0.0015)	(0.0036)	(0.0027)
Milk products	2.10	0.42	-7.13
	(0.0018)	(0.0004)	(0.0062)
Low-fat milk products	-1.50	-14.56	9.49
	(0.0013)	(0.0125)	(0.0082)
Diet drinks	-2.59	8.94	-4.88
	(0.0032)	(0.0110)	(0.0060)
Nondiet drinks	-3.31	5.40	-7.17
	(0.0360)	(0.0587)	(0.0779)

All coefficients are statistically significant at 1% level. LILA - Low-income, low-access.
Source: Computed by USDA, Economic Research Service.

Table 7
Effect on food purchases of living in rural and urban low-income, low-access areas 2

	Urban	Rural LILA	Urban LILA	Rural LILA * distance	Urban LILA * distance	distance	Urban * distance
Fruits	12.37	4.01	-9.52	-0.30	0.55	0.16	-0.62
	(0.0049)	(0.0016)	(0.0037)	(0.0001)	(0.0002)	(0.0001)	(0.0002)
Vegetables	3.71	0.43	-9.14	0.20	0.79	-0.04	0.11
	(0.0027)	(0.0003)	(0.0066)	(0.0001)	(0.0006)	(0.0000)	(0.0001)
Sweets	-0.01	7.47	0.20	-0.54	-0.09	0.04	-0.15
	(0.0000)	(0.0061)	(0.0002)	(0.0004)	(0.0001)	(0.0000)	(0.0001)
Oils, nuts	3.24	13.59	-8.28	-0.69	0.89	0.96	-0.32
	(0.0027)	(0.0115)	(0.0070)	(0.0006)	(0.0008)	(0.0008)	(0.0003)
Eggs	-5.71	-0.18	7.73	0.04	-0.52	-0.13	0.18
	(0.0018)	(0.0001)	(0.0024)	(0.0000)	(0.0002)	(0.0000)	(0.0001)
Red meats	-22.47	5.94	9.22	0.02	0.16	-0.27	0.74
	(0.0234)	(0.0062)	(0.0096)	(0.0000)	(0.0002)	(0.0003)	(0.0008)
Low-fat red meats	-22.17	10.89	-0.38	-0.50	1.33	-1.70	1.51
	(0.0573)	(0.0281)	(0.0010)	(0.0013)	(0.0034)	(0.0044)	(0.0039)
Fish, poultry	5.42	3.46	-5.23	0.23	0.56	0.62	-0.38
	(0.0125)	(0.0080)	(0.0120)	(0.0005)	(0.0013)	(0.0014)	(0.0009)
Processed foods	2.11	-4.34	2.62	0.22	-0.27	-0.12	0.11
	(0.0062)	(0.0128)	(0.0077)	(0.0007)	(0.0008)	(0.0003)	(0.0003)
Grains	-4.34	-1.79	-1.59	0.08	-0.33	-0.18	0.21
	(0.0047)	(0.0020)	(0.0017)	(0.0001)	(0.0004)	(0.0002)	(0.0002)
Milk products	-7.30	-1.91	0.24	0.29	0.03	0.09	0.11
	(0.0064)	(0.0017)	(0.0002)	(0.0002)	(0.0000)	(0.0001)	(0.0001)
Low-fat milk products	8.20	-2.91	-14.18	0.21	-0.06	-0.38	-0.06
	(0.0071)	(0.0025)	(0.0123)	(0.0002)	(0.0001)	(0.0003)	(0.0001)
Diet drinks	-1.22	0.56	9.20	-0.37	-0.05	0.47	-0.32
	(0.0015)	(0.0007)	(0.0113)	(0.0005)	(0.0001)	(0.0006)	(0.0004)
Nondiet drinks	-3.82	-3.51	7.14	-0.06	-0.32	0.26	-0.43
	(0.0415)	(0.0382)	(0.0776)	(0.0006)	(0.0035)	(0.0029)	(0.0047)

All coefficients are statistically significant at 1% level. LILA - Low-income, low-access.
Source: Computed by USDA, Economic Research Service.

Table 8
Effect of distance and low income on food purchases

	Urban	Poor	Mile 1/urban	Mile 10/rural	LILA/urban	LILA/rural
Fruits	11.28	-5.72	-7.25	6.21	-0.96	3.42
	(0.0045)	(0.0023)	(0.0029)	(0.0025)	(0.0004)	(0.0014)
Vegetables	4.40	-2.71	-0.45	0.25	-2.69	4.73
	(0.0032)	(0.0019)	(0.0003)	(0.0002)	(0.0019)	(0.0034)
Sweets	-1.28	2.59	0.14	-12.89	-2.41	1.72
	(0.0010)	(0.0021)	(0.0001)	(0.0104)	(0.0020)	(0.0014)
Oils, nuts	-2.26	-1.58	1.09	21.90	-2.40	4.30
	(0.0019)	(0.0013)	(0.0009)	(0.0187)	(0.0021)	(0.0037)
Eggs	-4.85	0.37	0.87	-6.46	4.59	1.05
	(0.0015)	(0.0001)	(0.0003)	(0.0020)	(0.0014)	(0.0003)
Red meats	-21.61	5.99	11.09	0.77	3.63	0.67
	(0.0223)	(0.0062)	(0.0114)	(0.0008)	(0.0037)	(0.0007)
Low-fat red meats	-12.50	0.97	12.14	-6.19	4.10	-0.87
	(0.0321)	(0.0025)	(0.0312)	(0.0159)	(0.0105)	(0.0022)
Fish, poultry	0.24	3.10	5.05	31.83	-5.54	-0.77
	(0.0005)	(0.0071)	(0.0116)	(0.0733)	(0.0127)	(0.0018)
Processed foods	3.60	-0.09	-1.14	-1.73	1.42	-1.44
	(0.0106)	(0.0003)	(0.0034)	(0.0051)	(0.0042)	(0.0042)
Grains	-4.47	-2.90	3.91	-1.20	-1.59	0.95
	(0.0049)	(0.0032)	(0.0043)	(0.0013)	(0.0017)	(0.0010)
Milk products	-7.49	1.07	2.54	15.19	-0.82	-2.06
	(0.0065)	(0.0009)	(0.0022)	(0.0132)	(0.0007)	(0.0018)
Low-fat milk products	9.68	-15.07	-4.23	-3.09	-1.66	10.13
	(0.0083)	(0.0129)	(0.0036)	(0.0026)	(0.0014)	(0.0087)
Diet drinks	-6.60	2.42	4.23	-3.53	6.37	-3.60
	(0.0081)	(0.0030)	(0.0052)	(0.0043)	(0.0078)	(0.0044)
Nondiet drinks	-3.39	9.93	-6.83	-5.96	-1.69	-9.08
	(0.0368)	(0.1075)	(0.0740)	(0.0645)	(0.0183)	(0.0984)

All coefficients are statistically significant at 1% level. LILA - Low-income, low-access.
Source: Computed by USDA, Economic Research Service.

Store Channels and Their Effect on Food Purchases

There is little difference in the retail channels patronized by LILA and non-LILA consumers (LILA consumers purchase more from supercenters and non-LILA consumers purchase more from supermarkets), but it is possible that the same retail channels offer different products in LILA areas. In this section, we investigate whether LILA and non-LILA consumers buy similar products in the same retail channels. We include five retail channel indicators in the estimation, with grocery stores (the most popular channel) the omitted category.

Retail channel or format has a large effect on food purchases. Purchases in supercenters were associated with less healthful purchases. When consumers increase the share of expenditures in supercenter stores by 10 percentage points, this change is associated with an increases in purchases of low-fat meats (16 percent) and red meats (4.4 percent) and a decrease in purchases of fruits (2.5 percent) and vegetables (2.6 percent). Other store channels have average expenditure shares less than 10 percent, so we can reliably estimate only small changes to the expenditure share of these channels.

Explaining Food Disparities: Access or Preferences?

LILA consumers living far from supermarkets with limited means of transportation may face a food environment that makes it difficult to purchase healthy foods. In this report, we measured the effect of living in LILA areas on consumer food purchases. Consumers living in LILA areas consume fewer fruits, vegetables, and low-fat milk products and more red meats and drinks (diet and nondiet). The magnitudes of the differences are small and, even if eliminated, would not translate into significant dietary or health improvements. The effects of demographic variables—such as race, education, and income—on food purchases are much larger than the effect from living in a LILA area.

LILA consumers travel slightly farther from home to purchase their food. Almost all LILA households travel to stores more than 1 mile from their home, the distance commonly used to delineate low food access. Thus, of the 7.7 percent of households in the Homescan sample who lived in LILA areas, very few limited their food purchases to the LILA areas.

LILA consumers who travel farther to buy food purchase more fruits, vegetables, fish, and poultry and fewer drinks (diet and nondiet). Perhaps, stores close to LILA consumers sell a variety of products similar to those offered at convenience stores, such as drinks, milk, sweets, and limited meats and produce. When LILA consumers travel farther to retail stores that offer a greater variety of foods and they are unconstrained in their choices, LILA consumers exhibit stronger preferences for fish, poultry, and produce, but the magnitudes of these effects are small and they cannot explain large nutritional disparities observed in the population.

The LILA definition requires that a rural area be at least 10 miles from the nearest supermarket to be classified as a low food-access area. However, even with this generous parameter, food demand in rural LILA areas is hardly different from other rural areas. Rural residents generally tend to buy fewer healthy food products than urban consumers.

For an area to classify as LILA, it must have both limited access to supermarkets and low income levels. The poverty level of a census tract, we find, is a more important factor for unhealthy food purchases than is access to stores. Distance to retail foodstores has almost no effect on purchases in rural areas, but a small negative effect in urban areas.

If LILA consumers are restricted in their choice of stores and are compelled to shop in stores with high prices and a scarcity of healthy food, we would expect to see differences in the retail channels where LILA and non-LILA consumers shop. However, our results do not bear this out. Instead, the descriptive statistics of retail channels (table 1) show that the difference in retail channels patronized by LILA and non-LILA households is small. Thus, if we assume that stores in the same retail channel offer a similar variety of healthy foods, then there is little difference in the availability of healthy foods to LILA and non-LILA consumers. Nor do we find that LILA consumers are facing higher prices; in fact, they are facing slightly lower prices for most food products (see table 2).

After controlling for the retail channel where consumers shop (table 9), the baseline difference in food purchases between LILA and non-LILA households decreases by half. LILA consumers purchased less healthful food in all retail channels except supercenters compared to non-LILA consumers. On the other hand, LILA consumers purchased less healthful products in supermarkets and club stores, which tend to have the most healthful product offerings, suggesting lower preferences for these products among LILA consumers.

The relatively poor diet of LILA consumers cannot be explained by their inability to reach supermarkets or by different relative prices in supermarkets where they shop. Two likely explanations are that LILA consumers have different preferences than non-LILA consumers, or that LILA consumers shop in stores that offer a different variety of products than the stores where non-LILA consumers shop, even if these stores belong to the same retail channel. Future research examining the variety of products offered in the stores where LILA consumers shop may illuminate this issue.

Conclusion

Our results begin to shed light on whether the quality of food choices in low-access areas is a demand or supply problem. Do consumers in LILA areas value supermarkets less or do those retail outlets, for some reason, avoid these areas? We find that LILA area consumers purchase unhealthier food products than consumers living elsewhere. The difference in the healthfulness of their purchases, however, is quite small. Also, LILA area consumers tend not to purchase much healthier items farther from home, suggesting that these consumers exhibit less demand for such items. Households in LILA areas must travel unrealistically long distances to erase even the small disparity with non-LILA households in healthfulness of food purchases. Thus, as the effect of living in LILA areas on diets is modest, the dietary effect of a policy attracting supermarkets to these areas will be similarly modest.

There are three important caveats to our results. First, Nielsen HomeScan data underrepresent poor consumers. We correct this problem somewhat by using population weights, but this remedy cannot help if the poor in Homescan are systematically different from the poor not sampled by it. We suspect that the coverage of the very poor may be particularly lacking. Second, our match of store locations to consumers is imperfect, which introduces a measurement error to our distance variable for the unmatched stores. Finally, we observe the food purchased in stores only to the extent that participants correctly report it, and we don't have information on food consumed away from home in restaurants, schools, and other places, which are important components of overall food consumption.

While these caveats may be daunting, this is the best data available at the moment that links food purchases with consumer and store locations. In addition, this study benefits from a large consumer panel with frequent and detailed information on food purchases. The fact that this is the first large national study of food purchases in LILA areas illustrates the data difficulties faced by researchers. Future research might combine a better measurement of food consumed away from home with better coverage of poor consumers. USDA's National Household Food Acquisition and Purchase Survey (FoodAPS), recently available, combines both and is an attractive avenue for future research on food access and food purchases.

Our results show that living in LILA areas does not have major adverse effects on the food purchases for most residents of these areas. At the same time, given our data limitations, it is possible that living in LILA areas is a large problem for a small minority of particularly disadvantaged consumers. Future research with a better coverage of the very poor consumers can shed light on this question.

Appendix

Calculating Elasticity: Price Elasticity of Demand

In the fully interactive EASI model we estimate

$$w^j = \sum_{r=1}^{R} b_r^j y^r + \sum_{t=1}^{T} g_t^j z_t + \sum_{k=1}^{J} a_n^{jk} \ln p^k + \sum_{t=1}^{T} \sum_{k=1}^{J} c^{jkt} z_t \ln p^k +$$

$$\sum_{k=1}^{J} d_n^{jk} \ln p^k y + \sum_{t=1}^{T} h_t^j z_t y + \varepsilon^j \qquad (2)$$

Hicksian price semi-elasticity

$$\frac{\partial w_j}{\partial \ln p_k} = a_n^{jk} + \sum_{t=1}^{T} z_t c^{jkt} + \sum_{l=0}^{L} A_{lji} z_l + d_n^{jk} y \qquad (3)$$

From Hicksian semi-elasticity we can calculate Hicksian elasticity:

$$\frac{\partial w_i}{\partial \ln p_j} = \frac{\partial \left[\frac{q_i^h p_j}{x^h} \right]}{\partial \ln p_i} = \frac{\partial q_i^h}{\partial \ln p_j} \frac{p_i}{x^h} + \frac{\partial p_i}{\partial \ln p_j} \frac{q_i^h}{x^h} - \frac{q_i^h p_i}{\left(x^h \right)^2} \frac{\partial x^h}{\partial \ln p_j}$$

$$= \frac{\partial q_i^h}{\partial \ln p_j} \frac{q_i^h}{q_i^h} \frac{p_i}{x^h} + \frac{\partial p_i}{\partial \ln p_j} \frac{p_i}{p_i} \frac{q_i^h}{x^h} - \frac{q_i^h p_i}{\left(x^h \right)^2} \frac{\partial x^h}{\partial p_j} \frac{p_j}{1}$$

$$= \frac{\partial \ln q_i^h}{\partial \ln p_j} w_i^h + \frac{\partial \ln p_i}{\partial \ln p_j} \frac{q_i^h p_i}{x^h} - \frac{q_i^h p_i}{x^h} \frac{q_j^h p_j}{x^h}$$

$$= \frac{\partial \ln q_i^h}{\partial \ln p_j} w_i^h + 1_{ij} w_i^h - w_i^h w_j^h$$

Then the Hicksian elasticity is

$$h_{ij} = \frac{\partial \ln q_i^h}{\partial \ln p_j} = \frac{\partial w_i}{w_i^h \partial \ln p_j} + w_j^h - 1_{ij}$$

Where $1_{ij} = 1$ if $i = j$ and $1_{ij} = 0$ if $i \neq j$.

From equation (2) we can derive Marshallian expenditure semi-elasticity (see details in the Appendix of Lewbel and Pendakur (2009)) where $x^m x^m$ is the Marshallian expenditures.

From the semi-elasticity we can derive elasticity:

$$\frac{\partial w_i}{\partial \ln x^m} = \frac{\partial \left[\frac{q_i^m p_j}{x^m} \right]}{\partial \ln x^m} = \frac{\partial q_i^m}{\partial x} \frac{x^m p_i}{x^m} + \frac{\partial \left(\frac{1}{x^m} \right)}{\partial x^m} \frac{p_i q_i^m x^m}{1}$$

$$\frac{\partial w_i}{\partial \ln x^m} = \frac{\partial q_i^m}{\partial x} \frac{x^m}{q_i^m} \frac{p_i q_i^m}{x_m} + \frac{p_i q_i^m x^m}{\left(x^m \right)^2}$$

$$e_i = \frac{\partial q_i^m}{\partial x} \frac{x^m}{q_i^m} = \frac{\partial w_i}{w_i \partial \ln x^m} + 1$$

From Slutsky's equation for elasticities

$$e_{ij} = h_{ij} - w_j e_i$$

we can derive Marshallian price elasticities:

$$e_{ij} = \frac{\partial w_i}{w_i^h \partial \ln p_j} + w_j^h - 1_{ij} - w_j \left(\frac{\partial w_i}{w_i \partial \ln x^m} + 1 \right)$$

Elasticity with respect to Z's

Lewbel and Pendakur (2009) present a general formula for budget semi-elasticity:

$$\nabla_z w \left(p, x, z, \varepsilon \right) = \left[I_J + \nabla_y w \left(p, y, z, \varepsilon \right) P' \right]^{-1} \left[\nabla_z w \left(p, y, z, \varepsilon \right) \right]$$

From (2) we know that:

$$\nabla_z w \left(p, y, z, \varepsilon \right) = \frac{\partial w_j}{\partial z_t} = g_t^j + \sum_{k=1}^{J} c^{jkt} \ln p^k + h_t^j y \quad and \quad \nabla_y w \left(p, y, z, \varepsilon \right) = \frac{\partial w_j}{\partial y} =$$

$$r \sum_{r=1}^{R} b_r^j y^{r-1} + \sum_{k=1}^{J} d_n^{jk} \ln p^k y + \sum_{t=1}^{T} h_t^j z_t$$

and ..

Then a budget semi-elasticity with respect to z's is:

$$\frac{\partial w_j(p,x,z,\varepsilon)}{\partial z_t} = \frac{r\sum_{r=1}^{R} b_r^j y^{r-1} + \sum_{k=1}^{J} d_n^{jk} \ln p^k y + \sum_{t=1}^{T} h_t^j z_t}{1 + g_t^j + \sum_{k=1}^{J} c^{jkt} \ln p^k + h_t^j y}$$

Next we find the quantity elasticity of demand with respect to z's:

$$\frac{\partial \ln q_j}{\partial z_t} = \frac{\partial q_j}{\partial z_t}\frac{1}{q_j} = \frac{\partial \frac{w_j x}{p_j}}{\partial z_t}\frac{1}{\frac{w_j x}{p_j}}$$

As total spending and market prices do not depend on z variables:

$$\frac{\partial x}{\partial z_t} = 0 \, , \frac{\partial p_j}{\partial z_t} = 0$$

Then the quantity elasticity of demand with respect to z's is:

$$\frac{\partial \ln q_j}{\partial z_t} = \frac{\partial w_j}{\partial z_t}\frac{x}{p_j}\frac{p_j}{w_j x} = \frac{1}{w_j}\frac{\partial w_j}{\partial z_t}$$

Appendix table 1

Robustness check: OLS estimated expenditures (percent)

	Budget share of fruits	Budget share of vegetables
LILA	-2.93***	-5.31***
	(0.77)	(0.93)
LILA	-5.92***	-7.36***
	(1.17)	(1.41)
Dist_w	-0.012	-0.34***
	(0.042)	(0.051)
LILA * distance	0.39	0.34**
	(0.18)	(0.15)

Coefficients statistically significant at 1% level are marked bold. LILA = Low-income, low-access. OLS = Ordinary Least Squares.
Source: Computed by USDA, Economic Research Service.

References

Amemiya, T. (1979). "The estimation of a simultaneous-equation Tobit model," *International Economic Review*: 169-181.

Anderson, M. L., and D. A. Matsa (2011). "Are restaurants really supersizing America?" *American Economic Journal: Applied Economics* 152-188.

Aussenberg, R. A. (2014). *SNAP and Related Nutrition Provisions of the 2014 Farm Bill* (P.L. 113-79), Congressional Research Service Report.

Beaulac, J., E. Kristjansson, and S. Cummins (2009). "Peer Reviewed: A Systematic Review of Food Deserts, 1966-2007," *Preventing Chronic Disease* 6(3).

Block, D., and J. Kouba (2006). "A comparison of the availability and affordability of a market basket in two communities in the Chicago area," *Public Health Nutrition* 9(07): 837-845.

Broda, C., E. Leibtag, and D. E. Weinstein (2009). "The role of prices in measuring the poor's living standards," *The Journal of Economic Perspectives* 23(2): 77-97.

Chen, S., R. J. Florax, S. Snyder, and C. C. Miller (2010). "Obesity and access to chain grocers," *Economic Geography* 86(4): 431-452.

Chen, S.E., R.J. Florax, and S.D. Snyder (2013). "Obesity and fast food in urban markets: a new approach using geo-referenced micro data," *Health Economics* 22(7): 835-856.

Chung, C., and S.L. Myers (1999). "Do the poor pay more for food? An analysis of grocery store availability and food price disparities," *Journal of Consumer Affairs* 33(2): 276-296.

Cummins, S., E. Flint, and S.A. Matthews (2014). "New neighborhood grocery store increased awareness of food access but did not alter dietary habits or obesity,." *Health Affairs* 33(2): 283-291.

Diewert, W. E. (1976). "Exact and superlative index numbers," *Journal of Econometrics* 4(2): 115-145.

Dutko, Paula, Michele Ver Ploeg, and Tracey Farrigan. *Characteristics and Influential Factors of Food Deserts,* ERR-140, U.S. Department of Agriculture, Economic Research Service, August 2012

Edin, K., M. Boyd, J. Mabli, J. Ohls, J. Worthington, S. Greene, N. Redel, and S. Sridharan (2013). SNAP Food Security In-Depth Interview Study, Mathematica Policy Research.

Einav, L., E. Leibtag, and A. Nevo (2008). *On the Accuracy of Nielsen Homescan Data.* U.S. Department of Agriculture, Economic Research Service. ERR-69

Einav, L., E. Leibtag, and A. Nevo (2010). "Recording discrepancies in Nielsen Homescan data: Are they present and do they matter?" Quant Marc Econ 8(2): 207-239.

Ford, P. B., and D. A. Dzewaltowski (2008). "Disparities in obesity prevalence due to variation in the retail food environment: three testable hypotheses,." *Nutrition Reviews* 66(4): 216-228.

Holsten, J. E. (2009). "Obesity and the community food environment: a systematic review," *Public Health Nutrition* 12(03): 397-405.

Horowitz, C. R., K. A. Colson, P. L. Hebert, and K. Lancaster (2004). "Barriers to buying healthy foods for people with diabetes: evidence of environmental disparities," *American Journal of Public Health* 94(9).

Lewbel, A., and K. Pendakur (2009). "Tricks with Hicks: The EASI demand system," *The American Economic Review*: 827-863.

Lin, B.-H., M. Ver Ploeg, P. Kasteridis, and S. T. Yen (2014). "The roles of food prices and food access in determining food purchases of low-income households," *Journal of Policy Modeling* 36(5): 938-952.

Maryland House Bill 451 (2014). Neighborhood Business Development Program - Financial Assistance for Food Deserts. HB 451. Maryland General Assembly, Department of Legislative Services: 1-7.

Moore, L. V., and A. V. Diez Roux (2006). "Associations of neighborhood characteristics with the location and type of food stores," *American Journal of Public Health* 96(2): 325-331.

Moore, L. V., A. V. D. Roux, J. A. Nettleton, and D. R. Jacobs (2008). "Associations of the Local Food Environment with Diet Quality—A Comparison of Assessments Based on Surveys and Geographic Information Systems: The Multi-Ethnic Study of Atherosclerosis." *American Journal of Epidemiology* 167(8): 917-924.

Morland, K., A. V. Diez Roux, and S. Wing (2006). "Supermarkets, other food stores, and obesity: the atherosclerosis risk in communities study," *American Journal of Preventive Medicine* 30(4): 333-339.

Morland, K., S. Wing, A. Diez Roux, and C. Poole (2002). "Neighborhood characteristics associated with the location of food stores and food service places," *American Journal of Preventive Medicine* 22(1): 23-29.

Newey, W. K. (1987). "Efficient estimation of limited dependent variable models with endogenous explanatory variables," *Journal of Econometrics* 36(3): 231-250.

Park, C. W., E. S. Iyer, and D. C. Smith (1989). "The effects of situational factors on in-store grocery shopping behavior: the role of store environment and time available for shopping," *Journal of Consumer Research*: 422-433.

Pearson, T., J. Russell, M. J. Campbell, and M. E. Barker (2005). "Do 'food deserts' influence fruit and vegetable consumption?—A cross-sectional study," *Appetite* 45(2): 195-197.

Rose, D., and R. Richards (2004). "Food store access and household fruit and vegetable use among participants in the US Food Stamp Program," *Public Health Nutrition* 7(08): 1081-1088.

Sharkey, J. R., C. M. Johnson, and W. R. Dean (2010). "Food access and perceptions of the community and household food environment as correlates of fruit and vegetable intake among rural seniors," *BMC Geriatrics* 10(1): 32.

U.S. Centers for Disease Control and Prevention (2012). *State Initiatives Supporting Healthier Food Retail: An Overview of the National Landscape*, National Center for Chronic Disease Prevention and Health Promotion: 1-10. U.S. Department of Agriculture (2015). "Food Access Research Atlas."

U.S. Department of Labor, Bureau of Labor Statistics (2011). *Consumer Expenditures - 2010.* USDL-11-1395.

Ver Ploeg, V. Breneman, T. Farrigan, K. Hamrick, D. Hopkins, P. Kaufman, B.-H. Lin, M. Nord, T. Smith, and R. Williams (2009). "Access to affordable and nutritious food: measuring and understanding food deserts and their consequences." Report to Congress. USDA, Economic Research Service.

Ver Ploeg, Michele, Vince Breneman, Paula Dutko, Ryan Williams, Samantha Snyder, Chris Dicken, and Phil Kaufman (2012). *Access to Affordable and Nutritious Food: Updated Estimates of Distance to Supermarkets Using 2010 Data*, ERR-143, U.S. Department of Agriculture, Economic Research Service, Nov.

Volpe, R., A. Okrent, and E. Leibtag (2013). "The effect of supercenter-format stores on the healthfulness of consumers' grocery purchases," *American Journal of Agricultural Economics* 95(3).

Wilde, P., J. Llobrera, and M. Ver Ploeg (2014). "Population Density, Poverty, and Food Retail Access in the United States: An Empirical Approach," *International Food and Agribusiness Management Review,*

Volume 17, Special Issue A.

Zhen, C., E. A. Finkelstein, J. M. Nonnemaker, S. A. Karns, and J. E. Todd (2013). "Predicting the effects of sugar-sweetened beverage taxes on food and beverage demand in a large demand system," *American Journal of Agricultural Economics* 96(1).

Zhen, C., M. K. Wohlgenant, S. Karns, and P. Kaufman (2010). "Habit formation and demand for sugar-sweetened beverages," *American Journal of Agricultural Economics* 93(1).

www.ingramcontent.com/pod-product-compliance
Lightning Source LLC
Chambersburg PA
CBHW081134280526

45787CB00007B/3082